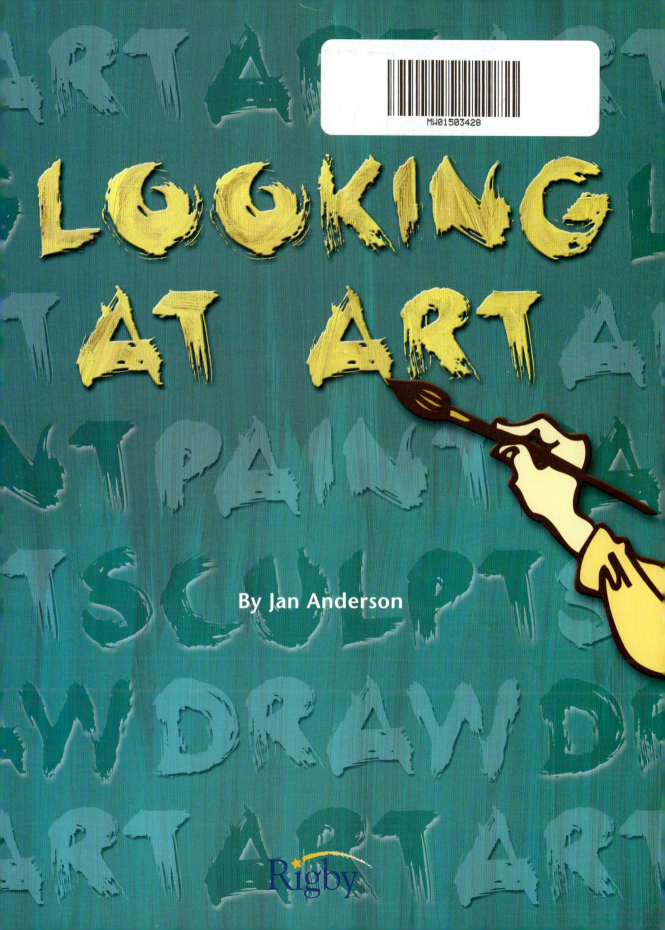

LOOKING AT ART

By Jan Anderson

Rigby

Rigby PM Plus Nonfiction
part of the Rigby PM Program
Emerald Level

U.S. edition © 2003 Rigby Education
A division of Reed Elsevier Inc.
1000 Hart Road
Barrington, IL 60010 - 2627
www.rigby.com

Text © 2003 Thomson Learning Australia
Illustrations © 2003 Thomson Learning Australia
Originally published in Australia by Thomson Learning Australia

10 9 8 7 6 5 4 3 2 1
07 06 05 04 03

Looking at Art
  ISBN 0 7578 4216 0

Printed in China by Midas Printing (Asia) Ltd

Photographs by **AAP Image**, pp. 22, 23, 18 bottom left; **Australian Picture Library/
Corbis**, p. 20 top/ Archivo Iconograffico, p. 14/ Barney Burstein, p. 20 bottom/ Bettermann,
p. 19/ Charles & Josette Lenars, pp. 6 top, 18 top/ Christie's Images, pp. 4 top, 9 bottom/
Cuchi White, p. 17 top/ Dave G. White, p. 7 center/ David Lees, pp. 12, 13 top/ Franz-Mark
Frei, p. 6 bottom/ Gail Mooney, p. 18 bottom right/ Gianni Dagli, p. 9 top/ Michael Freeman,
p. 7 top/ Ted Spiegel, p. 17 bottom/ World Films Enterprise, p. 15 top; **Lindsay Edwards**,
cover, pp. 21; **Getty Images**/ The Image Bank, p. 15 bottom; **National Gallery of
Australia**/ attributed to Jacaob Gerritsz Cuyp, Portait of Abel Tasman, his wife and
daughter, c.1640s, oil on canvas, 106.7 x 132.1 cm, Rex Nan Kivell Collection courtesy of
the National Library of Australia and National Gallery of Australia, Canberra, pp. 11 left,
11 right, 13 bottom; **National Library of Australia**, p. 16; **Photoedit**/ Michael Newman,
p. 5 top; **Photolibrary.com**/ Science Photo Library/ James Stevenson, p. 10; **The Art
Archive**/ Dagli Orti, p. 4 bottom/ Victoria and Albert Museum London/ Sally Chapell, p. 8.

Contents

CHAPTER 1

Art Around Us

Art is an important part of our lives. It affects us in many different ways.

Paintings and sculpture can make us feel happy, or calm. When artists paint pictures, they show their thoughts and feelings in a way that they could not do with words. That's why some works of art can puzzle us, or even make us laugh.

The Sun of Man
by René Magritte

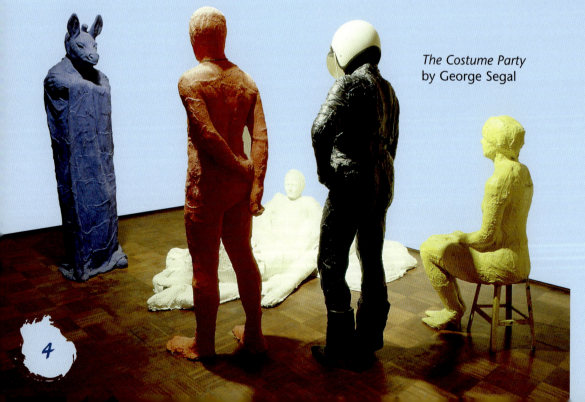

The Costume Party
by George Segal

Technology is becoming an important part of art. Some artists use computers to help them make pictures. Other artists use videos as part of their **installations**, a type of modern sculpture.

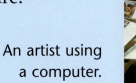
An artist using a computer.

Technology can also help art museums look after their works of art. There are special machines that check the air in a museum to make sure that it is not too hot, or too moist, for the paintings.

X-ray photos of a painting can sometimes show how it was made. Other kinds of technology can show whether a painting is an original or a copy.

Did You Know?

Many paintings are now bought and sold in **cyberspace** — on the Internet.

CHAPTER 2

The Arts, Past and Present

The first artists were probably the people who painted pictures on the walls of caves. Art, and the materials used to create it, have changed over time.

For many years, wood was used as a surface on which to paint. Paper and **canvas** then became popular surfaces for painting. Canvas is a kind of cloth that is made of linen or cotton. The canvas is stretched across a wooden frame.

Artists like to paint on canvas. Oil paint sticks well to the canvas, and the texture of the cloth looks good through the paint.

Many old sculptures were made of stone. Later they were made of metals and **alloys** like **bronze**.

Today, artists have many more kinds of material that they can make into interesting sculptures. Some artists like to work with **plastic**, and many of them use all kinds of recycled materials.

Cowboy sculptures made from recycled materials.

Did You Know?

Photography with digital cameras has become a popular kind of art. The pictures can be changed on the computer, so the final picture can be very different from the original photo.

CHAPTER 3

Paints over the Years

All paints contain a **pigment**. Pigments are substances that give paints their colors. The first pigments came from the earth or from plants. Today, pigments can also be made in factories. They are manufactured or **synthetic**.

The oldest kinds of paints are watercolors and oil paints. Most paintings in art museums were made using these.

The pigment in watercolor paints is held together with a gum taken from plants. The paint is thinned with water.

The English artist Joseph Turner was famous for his watercolor paintings of **landscapes**. This painting is called *Lake Brienz*.

In oil paints, the pigment is kept together with linseed oil, which also comes from a plant. The paint can be thinned with more oil.

This famous **portrait** by Leonardo da Vinci is called '*Mona Lisa*'. It is painted with oils.

'Gauguin's Chair' by David Hockney

The newest kinds of paints are **acrylics**. Artists first used them around 50 years ago. They are synthetic paints, in which the pigment is held together with a liquid plastic. The paint is thinned with liquid plastic, or even water.

Did You Know?

Some old kinds of paint were made from egg yolks or egg whites. This paint is called tempera.

9

CHAPTER 4

Technology and Art

Technology is used in art museums in many different ways. Museums have special machines to check changes in the air during the day.

This is important because when the air is too damp, mold can grow on the paintings, and make spots on them. When the air is too hot, cracks can form in oil paintings.

This machine makes graphs of the air temperature, and shows how much moisture is in the air. It is called a **thermohydrograph**.

This graph shows the temperature.

This graph shows the moisture in the air.

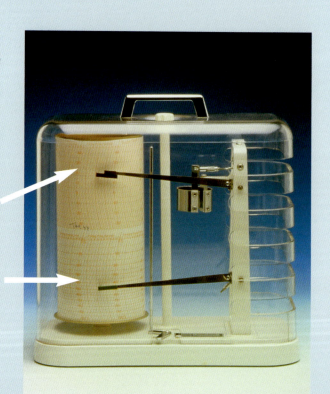

Some artists change their paintings many times as they work. The finished painting often looks very different to how it appeared at first. Other artists use their old paintings as a surface for painting new pictures. This saves them from buying new canvases, or boards. And sometimes artists paint over old pictures just because they do not like them!

With technology, art historians can use X-rays to look at the layers of paint that are under the surface of a painting. This tells us if a painting was changed, and how it was changed.

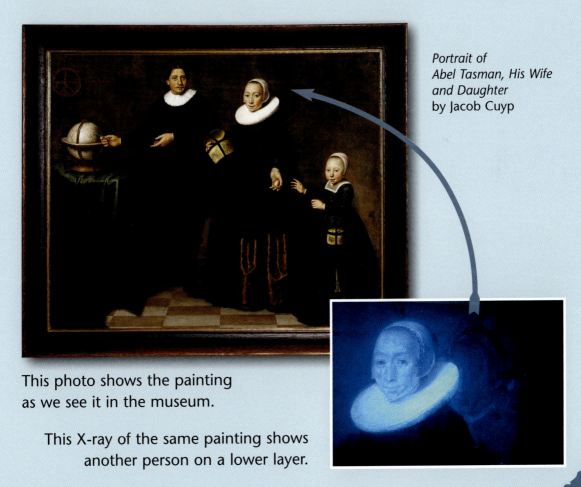

Portrait of Abel Tasman, His Wife and Daughter by Jacob Cuyp

This photo shows the painting as we see it in the museum.

This X-ray of the same painting shows another person on a lower layer.

CHAPTER 5

Cleaning Paintings

In the past, paintings were mostly cleaned by hand.

Scalpels, which are like small knives, were used to carefully scrape away small areas of dust. Special liquids were used on small pieces of soft material like cotton wool, to dissolve dirt that had built up on the surfaces of paintings. These methods are still used today.

Now, lasers are sometimes used instead. Laser machines make a beam of light that can be focused on a very small part of a painting, where there is dirt.

This means that dirt can be removed with less chance of hurting the painting.

Did You Know?

You must never touch a painting in a museum. Oils and sweat in your skin can harm the paint.

This man works in a museum. He is carefully restoring some areas of a very old painting. Before he started work, the painting was examined with special microscopes and magnifying glasses. This made it easier to find cracks in the surface, or places where the paint had fallen off, or faded.

After

Before

This close-up of the family portrait from page 11 shows how different a painting looks after the old, discolored varnish has been removed.

CHAPTER 6

Taking the Studio Outside

About 100 years ago, there was a famous group of painters called the Impressionists. They were more interested in painting **impressions** of everyday life than in making exact copies of what they saw.

These painters often left their studios to paint outside, in the open.

Monet liked to paint from his boat on a river. In *The Bridge at Argenteuil*, you can almost feel the ripples in the water.

The Impressionists were interested in the effect of light on the landscape. Some made thick strokes with their brushes, while others used small dabs of paint. They often used strong colors.

When artists' equipment became more **portable**, artists could paint almost anywhere.

Portable easels were small, foldable, and easy to carry. They could be taken to places far from home and set up in the countryside. Impressionists liked to paint this way.

Claude Monet and His Wife in His Floating Studio by Edouard Manet

In this painting, we can see an artist using a portable easel.

Metal tubes of paint were first made about 150 years ago. These were good for storing oil paints because the paint did not dry out inside the tube. Artists could carry their paints almost anywhere.

CHAPTER 7

Wall Paintings

Artists do not always paint on pieces of wood, paper, or canvas. They sometimes make pictures on walls, just like the cave painters of long ago.

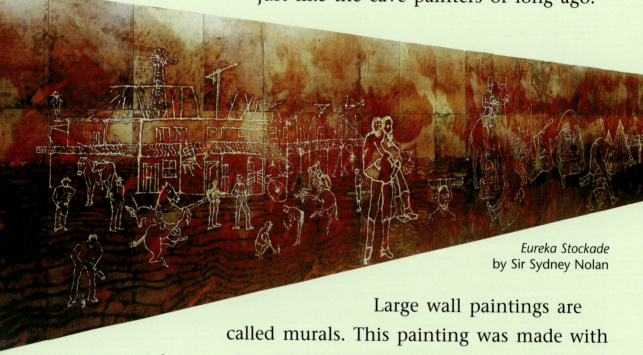

Eureka Stockade
by Sir Sydney Nolan

Large wall paintings are called murals. This painting was made with special materials called **enamels**. Enamels use very old technology. They were invented hundreds of years ago.

For this mural the artist made an outline of the drawing in enamel, on sheets of metal. He did the outline with his finger and thumb. The picture was so big that two other people had to help him paint. The sheets of metal were baked twice in a huge oven to get the colors that the artist wanted.

This painting on a wall looks like a real archway. However, it is really just a painting. The arch and houses look almost **three-dimensional** until you come close to them.

A fresco is the name we give to a painting that has been done on a plaster wall or ceiling, inside a building. The plaster absorbs the pigments in the paint.

This famous fresco called 'The School of Athens' was painted by the Italian artist Raphael.

Did You Know?

Some artists who paint murals buy their acrylic paint in spray cans. This way they can paint large areas much more quickly than by using brushes.

CHAPTER 8

Sculptures

A sculpture is a three-dimensional piece of art that has been carved, or shaped, using some kind of material. Very old sculptures were made of stone or wood.

These sculptures on Easter Island are made of stone.

The sculpture below is made of bronze.

After people learned how to make bronze from copper and tin, they used this material for sculptures.

Paper can also be used to create interesting sculptures.

Unusual sculptures

Christo is a famous artist who makes very different kinds of sculptures. He wraps up buildings and the landscape to make art. He does drawings and models of his sculptures before he makes them.

Christo needs strong materials that will not rip or rot when they are left outside. That is why he uses synthetic materials for his wrapping.

One of Christo's sculptures is called 'Surrounded Islands'. The bright pink material is a kind of plastic. It floats on the water. It took Christo over three years to plan this work of art and put it in place.

Did You Know?

Cranes and ladders have been used to put some of Christo's art in place.

CHAPTER 9

Pop Art

Pop art is a very modern kind of art. It began around 50 years ago, when artists decided to use everyday objects to make art. They simply called these objects "found objects," and they included flags, tires, windows, old cars ... almost anything.

Sculpture by Claes Oldenburg

At first, people did not like pop art because it was so different. They did not believe that everyday objects, like typewriter erasers ...

or parts of comic strips ...

Varoom! by Roy Lichtenstein

were really works of art.

20

Make Your Own Pop Art Sculpture

You will need:

- a pencil and a small sheet of paper

- a flat piece of wood, or a sheet of cardboard, about three feet long and three feet wide

- strong glue

- waste/recycled materials, like old packages, cups, or any items that are being thrown out at home

- paints.

What to do:

- Draw a plan of your pop art sculpture.

- Start to glue the waste materials to the wood or cardboard, using your plan.

- Stand back from the sculpture from time to time, to see if you like it.

- Try moving small parts of the sculpture around to get the best look.

- Paint the sculpture, and give it a name.

Plan for Pop Art Sculpture.

21

CHAPTER 10

Installations

An installation is a very modern kind of sculpture that has to be put together in the museum itself. It usually has more than one part, and is set up by a team of people using the artist's plan.

Artists often use modern technology to make their installations. They use slides, video clips, lights that go on and off, recorded sounds, fans which move paper in the air, and even machines that make a smell! One artist used twelve live horses in his installation.

Dots Obsession - New Century 2000 by Yayoi Kusama

Installations are often designed for one particular museum space. They may be moved to another museum, but they might not be, or do, exactly the same thing the next time they are set up. After all …

An installation by Ernesto Neto

… an installation is meant to be an experience!

Glossary

acrylic   a special type of plastic

alloys   strong metals made of a mix of metals

bronze   a material made of copper and tin

canvas   a strong piece of cloth, for painting on

cyberspace   a virtual, or unreal, place on the Internet

enamel   a hard, shiny kind of paint that is often used on metal

impression   something that has an effect on your mind or on your feelings

installations   modern sculptures using special effects

landscape   a view, or picture, of the countryside

pigment   a substance that colors things

portable   able to be carried around or moved easily

plastic   a synthetic material, made from chemicals that come from oil

portrait   a picture of a person

synthetic   made by people, not natural

thermohydrograph   a machine that checks the air in museums

three-dimensional when something has depth, as well as width and height